ON THE EDGES OF
SLEEP

POEMS OF WAR AND MEMORY

Claude AnShin Thomas

Mary Esther, Florida

Oakwood Publishing, a division of
Zaltho Foundation, Inc.
550 Mary Esther Cutoff NW, PMB 319
Fort Walton Beach, FL. 32548
www.zaltho.org

Copyright © 2024 by Claude A. Thomas

Proceeds from the sale of this book will be donated
to the Zaltho Foundation.

All rights reserved. No part of this publication, including artwork, may be
reproduced in any form or by any means, electronic or physical, without
prior written permission from Oakwood Publishing or the Zaltho Founda-
tion, Inc.

Cover and interior design by Hilary Harkness

Library of Congress Control Number: 2024931846

ISBN hardcover 978-1-7362934-4-7
ISBN paperback 978-1-7362934-5-4
ISBN ebook 978-1-7362934-6-1

Also available in audiobook.

Contents

ON THE EDGES OF
SLEEP

POEMS OF WAR AND MEMORY

1

I
don't
know
when it
stopped,
this
scratching
inside
my skin,
or if
it indeed
is just
resting—
I wander
around
town streets
paved
with their
emptiness,
a shared
kinship—
I sit under
A street lamp
looking
into
a pothole,
committing
to an act
of concentration,
I
touch
the aching
of 1,000
years
of loss;
confronted
by
wide eyes
disappearing
into

surf,
slipping beneath
the
sea,
held
in its
depths
far from
my view,
never to be
touched
again
in loving
embrace
except
in
day dreams
and
nightmares,
I
cry—
if only
I
had been
a stronger
swimmer.

2

There are
sounds,
smells
and tastes—
traces of
you
floating
all through me,
poking
at my skin,
my memory,
my sensations,
and as I
sit still
in the movement
of thought
I can smell your hair
and
around the
corner of my eyes
catch a glimpse of you
smiling.

3

It seems
that I
must have
gone
for a walk
last night
in the quiet
cold
of Thoreau Street—
It seems that
I could hear your shadow crying
as it has for 10,000
lifetimes;
It seems as if
I knew
that
you were
somewhere
and I just
couldn't find you
so I held your
silent breathing
and wiped your tears
from
my face.

4

As I
write
another poem
my mind
whispers to me,
that
I can't write,
and when I
write
my mind
continues to whisper
that I'm
really being
dishonest
because my ears
have gone deaf
from the insistence
that it would
be better
if
I just cut off
my fingers,
and so by
writing
I risk
looking foolish
and I risk
amputation;
all of this is
wrapped up
in my want
to create
the perfect
image,
the one that
will show
the glow of you
and yet all
that
pours out of

me are
melancholic
memories of
sitting
on the couch
together
watching
the onset
of an
ice age.

5

As I watch
the television
my eyelids grow
weary of
the blue glow,
they decided,
without my consent
I might add,
to leave the room—
they did, however,
provide a subtle
invitation
to me
that
I could
accompany
them;
after some
very weak attempts
to persuade them
not to go
I accepted
their decision
to leave
and decided
to go with
them—
I reached with my
left hand,
index finger extended
and pressed the off button on the
remote,
the magical box
that controls
the blue
light
and
was abruptly
plunged into
darkness,

resting, sleeping,
visiting
all of the various realms that exist
behind closed
eyes—
after a period
of quiet
I heard a soft voice
singing;
with my
closed eyes
I looked around
for the source,
I wandered through
many spaces
in my attempts
and in the end
I was unsuccessful,
so I simply returned
to the couch
pulled the blanket up
around my chin,
tucked my feet under
a large pillow
and allowed myself
to just feel
the comfort
and at some point
just before daylight
I had the thought:
"perhaps we will meet
somehow again
in the special light
of the night realms."

6

It is a short distance
between
here and
somewhere else,
it is a
short distance
between life and
death,
it is a short distance
between
sanity and
madness—
only the smallest
of steps
decide our direction—
so many
misjudge the distance
and
step off
some kind of
edge
and wander blindly
for 10,000 years
through hell realms
not tasting the difference
between apples
and poison,
dying
terrible deaths
convinced
the whole time
that they are
really living.

7

I listened
to my mind
laughing
which took on an existence
separate
from an
ordinary whole
and in
an unordinary
circumstance
masquerading
a false belief
of independent;
during an unordinary
day
we witness
trees
blowing in the wind,
in the middle
of an ordinary
thought
a question arises—
are the trees
moving or is it the wind,
the mind whispers
first that
it is of course
the trees
that are moving,
then corrects itself
and says that
no,
it is the wind
that is
moving,
and then corrects
itself
and says that
no,
it is both

that are moving—
so in
the light
of an ordinary
moment
we can
discover
that in truth
neither
the wind
or the tree
is moving,
it is really only
the mind
that is
actually moving.

8

My brain
is thick
like
too old oil
in an unused
motorcycle
and so I thought
that
I would write
a poem
just to
see what
would come out—
while writing
and throughout
most days,
I wonder
where
will I meet
next,
in what nest,
and will
next permit me
to feast on
a delicacy
of hours?

9

I trip
over twisted
vines that
grow wild
in confusion
and I
realize
that
I often think
too much—
I drag
and
shuffle my
feet
rather than
pick them up,
and simply
place
them down
one after the
other.

10

Sitting on
a curb
comforting the
afternoon streets
of Mobile—
the sky is
gray
and the air
chills my
skin
through the
weave
of my
samu;
while waiting
outside
the tourist
information
center at
Fort Conde
I decided to
take
my
curiosity
around the place—
as I ascended the stairs
leading to
gun emplacements,
the sun
appeared
to generously
warm
my face
in the exact
spot
that my child's
soft cheek
once rested,
I took my small
finger and

wiped
tears
that noticed.

11

She
called me
on the
phone,
a friend
from another
time,
to talk
about her dream,
the one that
has her
trapped
in a
tormented
sleep—
she talked
about
her
efforts
to wake
up,
possessed
of the
idea,
that
upon her
awakening,
the torment,
the smell
of
him,
alcohol
seeping
through
his pores,
his stale breath
coating
the inside
of her
nostrils

like dead
food
forgotten
in some
deep corner
of the
refrigerator,
would be gone...
the feel
of
him,
her father,
withdrawing
from
her,
but not completely,
would be gone...
she
relaxed,
her clenched
eyes
open,
I could
feel
the color
seep
back into
her fingernails
at once
indistinguishable
from
the
white
rumpled
sheets
now soaked
with her
fear...
I tasted
her

wild eyed
gaze
flashing down
the
confused
length
of her,
I listened
to her
hands,
in
dull terror
clawing
away
at
the
spent
condom
absorbed
in her...
and then
a
time distorted
voice
crawling through
thick air
scratching
out the
words;
"it's all right
dearie,
it's all right,
you know
we love
you"—
I knew
the madness
of it,
her
mothers

voice,
whipping
her brain,
leaving
trails
of
dead blood
that moved
this friend
from another
time,
into
the light
of a fast
moving
train,
that
ties
her feet
to the tracks...
screaming
fear
sounds,
I
also
watched her
playing with the
thoughts
that
if
no one
hears
her,
the spent
semen
sticking
to her
thighs,
matting her
pubic hair

may
finally
disappear.

12

I wonder,
when
Sand dollars
grow,
do they
ever grow to
be sand
ten dollars
or
sand
50 dollars
or are they
always just
sand
dollars?

13

I have been
instructed
that to
practice
the way of
awakening
is to free ones
self from
attachment.
Calm the mind
then I
will certainly
discover
a mirror
that does
not reflect.
I have
been instructed
that if
I am not
careful
with this simple
truth
I might turn
brown and
then collapse,
drowning
as a too
soft,
over-watered
plant.

14

Resting in
an
afternoon
dream
of
emerald green
waves
sparkling,
I imagine
how the sun
might melt
as it meets
the glaciers
of Reykjavik
coming
down from the
mountains to
soak the
cold from its
soul
and drink hot
black
tea
rich
with honey
and milk,
and if I
listen,
listen real
close,
I can hear
the soft
sound of
breathing
between
these
letters.

15

I wonder
if you will
appear
tonight,
or where I
might find
you
among the words;
and then
somewhere in
my peripheral vision
I hear
the textured
sound
of your
laughter
amidst the conversation
of waves,
I turn
to look at you,
extend
my index finger,
and touch
the mother
of pearl
left behind
by the retreating
gulf,
reflecting
a Navarre
sunset.

16

As I
worked in
the garden
on Wednesday
there was
the faint smell
of
Vibernum
dancing
on a wind
that gently
ruffled
the green
leaves
which protected
its
sensual
white
flowers
from
the sun
whose presence
can burn
the unprotected
back of the neck—
walking deliberately
I approached
this gift
of nature,
extended
both of my hands
cradling this delicate
flower
breathing in
the sweet fragrance
of its petals
and kissed
it ever
so gently.

17

I stood
directly
in front of you
and opened
up my chest
exposing my
heart
which
usually stays
tightly
protected in
its place;
I stood directly
in front of you
and opened
up my chest
so that you could
really look
inside the
skin and bone
house of
me,
raw,
unprotected
and I
realized
just how
afraid
I am
of tall trees
in lightning
storms
and of
ghosts
in the night.

18

I want
to drive
my
truck fast—
I want to
ride my motorcycle
endlessly
into the sun—
I want to ride
my bicycle
until I can't find
my breath,
I want to
slow down
the onset
of breakfast—
for years,
for thousands
of years,
I have been
looking
for someone
to walk
with me
in the fullness
of a
luncheon
to which
I'm often invited
and quickly
tire
of eating alone;
for thousands
of years
I have been
looking for
someone
to walk with
me
in the dark

shadows
of a full eclipse—
today
it was
there,
the wondering
place—
the place
where
the question
asks
if anyone
has legs
that might be
strong enough?

19

Growing
up
in Western
Pennsylvania
I remember
being mesmerized
by
the
ice eyes
that would
appear
on
too cold
winter windows,
and then
my thoughts
drifted
to playing
in the snow,
rolling around
laughing
and putting
snow
down
each others
shirt,
throwing
snow balls,
and making
angel wings—
and when
we
are finished
playing
would you
be interested
in sitting
together
on the couch,
sharing

a cup of tea
and
watching
American
football
even if
it doesn't snow
in
Mary Esther.

20

When I
want to
talk with you
all night,
face to
face,
where
are you
right now
as I walk
down
the beach
searching for
your
footprints;
where are
you right
now
as I
close my
eyes
and
reach out
into
space
to touch
something
finding
only
the
mind print
everywhere,
all over me,
and I wonder
if all this
talking
about
body things
has
pushed

too far
into my dreams
leaving me
forever
with only
the fragrance
and sound
in my heart.

21

I taste
tears of
confusion,
I ache
at the
question
of safety,
the grasping
for fixed points,
wanting to know
what's next—
I feel it
this grasping,
in a quiet
crowd
arguing
the silence
of fear,
doubt,
and disillusion
crawling
through my
bones—
I think that
today
it would
be a
good idea
to go
for
a run.

22

The past
can
look through
me
examining
parts of
me,
private places,
and still
I seem
to be
not seen;
I stand in
the middle
of a crowded
ball room
in rags,
unbathed
for weeks,
my mouth
open,
my body
positioned,
knees bent,
thighs touching
my chest,
legs spread
in labors'
scream
to give
birth
to a voice
that is
still
born—
I look again
and
again
for the sound
or the

volume
that may untangle
the crowded
thoughts
trapped
in the phone—
what I
want
is to
sit
on the couch
or
a soft chair
in the corner
of your
new
office
and speak
to you
directly.

23

I make
noises
to sit
quietly
on a black
cushion
and was visited
by image
after image
each attempting
to identify
a particular
state of
of being—
I could hear
the drums of
marching bands
at half time
with their
heads
stretched
tight
piercing the night
with a particular
manic tension
and I could
feel the aching
of confusion
in my elbows
pinning my arms
to my side
as I watched
them all
helpless
one by one
fade from view
surrendering
to the
illusion
of another
moment.

24

I have
been sitting
in front
of
the wall
for lifetimes,
at least
10,000,
and tonight
I will do my
best to
paint it full—
the house
is very
quiet,
people are in
their
respective rooms
visiting those
night
places
that people
go to when
they close
their eyes,
and I am
quietly alone
save for the
endless ringing
in my ears;
I walked
through
the dark
quiet
blindly,
away from the
blue light
to my room,
and stood in
front of

the door
I knew just
where it
was
standing
but somehow
I got confused
by the
dark
reflecting.

25

Listening
to the
sound of the
highway
through
hearing aids
whose batteries
gave out yesterday,
every sound
was muted
and somehow
far away,
the other cars
and things
seemed hiding
as child like
under a pillow—
I put on
my turn signal
and moved to
my right
to pass
a too slow
explorer
and noticed that
I wanted to
move
so fast
that I
would become
light,
disappear
into all
colors,
and then
became afraid
that I was
just another
interesting
photograph,

a contrast
study
in shades
of gray.

26

Sitting
together
with
heaven
and earth
I wonder,
why do
we make reference
to them as separate;
I have never
seen
the point—
when I look
outside
I see trees
giving shade
to
houses,
the street
being supported
by the earth—
green
helping me
to breathe,
cars passing,
a squirrel
on the window
sill
brown eyes
sparkling,
and I can
not,
for the life
of me
see the
difference
between
heaven and
earth
in the

flow
of these moments,
the innocence
of sleep
that rests
in my
arms.

27

I went
for
a walk
in a
gentle
gulf rain
soaking through
levi's that
hung loosely
from
my waste;
it was
night
and my
long standing
companion
of the dark
was hiding
somewhere,
perhaps behind
the clouds—
I was coming
from the
cinema
having just
witnessed
13 days
of
war-greed
and
as I walked
I felt
a familiar
sensation,
a movement
of thought,
feeling
and time,
that
on this occasion

began
in my toes
like the
morphine
rush
of
battle
signs,
preparing me
for another
guerrilla attack
by the dead
memories
of
all those
who have ever
died
in any war
throughout space
and time—
I wondered,
as I walked
in
the rain,
how this
aching would
stand up to
the smell
of incense
and your gentle
song of
the bell.

28

I have
the experience
over and
over
and over—
I can see her,
windex-clearly,
bare footed,
in a
shear
flowered
dress,
flowing
a silver
mercedes
hood ornament,
a peculiar
symbol of peace,
resting
in the soft part
of her throat,
the part
that
the shaolin
teach as
the most vulnerable
to the
two-fingered strike,
kept there
by a thin band
of brown leather—
I watched her,
through my
dream self,
walk toward me,
brown eyes
burning,
and at last
she stood
directly

in front
of me,
a shy killer—
I prepared
for the
John Wayne embrace,
imagined
our chests
touching,
the wetness of
her lips,
our taste buds
sparkling
of each other
and
she spit in my
face,
the Vietnam kiss,
the boy soldier's
welcome
home—
perhaps our
on-going
liaison,
is Kshitigarba's
gift?

29

Aching
to the
bone
roots
I look for
you
in the spaces
between the
words,
I walk
in shadows,
embrace
memory
and listen
to
voices
coming through
the opposite part
of the phone
that we all
talk through—
this morning
these sounds
had the
quality
of soft
summer rain
against
the window,
the kind
that invites
you
out
for long
walks
and then
covers you
with its
warm,
wet,
kissing.

30

I was walking
high in
the mountains
and I heard
it,
I heard
it rumbling,
and I asked you
if you could
hear her voice,
loreli,
whose eyes,
filled with
tears
and silence,
speak to me
of a press into
destruction
or something—
with so little
protection
I hope that
there is
somewhere
safe to
place
her love
when
the wind,
rain
and lightening
come—
I can see
her
you know
with eyes
that you do not
have access
to,
I can

see her
so easily slip back
from what
she
struggled
to get,
slip back
abruptly
into a life
she never
expected
only to
live
again and
again—
her trap,
a
dream of
worlds
and ideas that
are just
so much dust,
and die there
of old age,
never
waking up.

31

Truth
listens
to no one
and
creates
its
own
reality
out of
bits
and pieces
of
broken
mirror
whose
silver
has been
scratched off,
reflecting
empty
images
that
only a repainting
can make
full,
stop looking
for something
that isn't,
see through
illusion—
there is
nothing
sacred to
realize
outside.

32

Through
the transference
of heavy
to
light
I hold you,
all of you,
while you
cry
and cry
and
cry,
I wonder
where
all the water
comes
from
and am
I a strong
enough swimmer
to not get
washed away
by the too
old sorrow
that doesn't
want to
and can't
be
stopped—
just now
if I could
look inside,
place my
hands
all through
you,
what
would I
find,
war shadows

hiding
the wounded,
or you
emerging
to
an embrace
that has
been waiting
patiently
to hold you
forever.

33

Sometimes
the weather
comes
from the
northeast
pushing
the sun out
of the
sky,
the air
grows cold
and the
green
maple,
oak
and sycamore
leaves
show their
bellies,
a soft pale
color;
I could
see the rain
coming up the
river,
thunder boiling,
I could see
the lightning's
tongue
licking at the
earth,
the trees,
randomly
leaving burnt
traces,
I felt so
helpless
not knowing
where
or when

it might strike
again—
I got caught
in the rain
and completely
soaked,
it passed,
the sun found
its way back,
dried my clothes
and warmed
me,
put its cheek
next to
mine
and
I wondered
for just a
brief
moment,
when will
it come again?

34

In the
Intimacy
of reflection
I breathe
your
incense,
a delicate
smell,
and taste
your
flower,
fragile,
still standing
long after
the castles,
cottages,
and
sand dunes
have been
swallowed
into a
storm's stomach—
I go to
the hospital
tomorrow
in robes
so that
my fear
can hide
under
my dress
with a picture
of you
pouring
the unsaid
words
into me.
In silence
this morning
your voice,

husky
having not
been used
somehow
for many
lifetimes
prodded me
to understand
in this moment
that I
would always
have to share
you
with this
other lover,
sleep,
who holds you
in dream's
embrace
close,
face
in
face,
so warm
through the
cold nights
of winter
when I am
but a spark
in some remote
portion
of
memory.

35

Early
this afternoon,
I checked
the caller
ID
and it read
"unavailable,"
another
telemarketer,
another
empty
voice
attempting
to
sell me
more
lies than
I
really need—
but for
some
reason
I reached
out
to
shake hands
with
the heartless
lover
who wanted
to
convince me
with
their
scripted moaning
to go shopping
for luxury
condo's
in the South
Bronx,

the voice
on the
other
end
said hello
and
I
immediately fell
down
on my knees
and
embraced
her
ankles.

36

As darkness
approaches
so do
those ancient
eastern smells,
sounds,
and tastes,
like the
water pouring
over niagra,
running wild,
collapsing
into itself;
listening
to the ringing
in my ears
I wonder,
where are
you this
night?
You
who collects
my attention,
did you ever
arrive
at the
place that
held O'halloran
hostage?
Or are you
still wandering
around
the
winter
silent night
streets
of
kiel,
trapped in
complicated

traffic
patterns,
left and right
turns
that seem
always
to lead
back
to the same point,
one way
streets
that take
you
further
and further
from
the place
you
want
to be?

37

There
are certain
natural laws
which
cannot
be
violated
without
consequences—
love,
if it is
love,
will by its
very nature
manifest
newly
in each
unprotected
moment,
unknown
to any
idea of itself,
while
love,
if it is not
love,
will by its
very nature
scream
or cry
very loudly
and throw
things
against the
wall
consuming
the attention
of
desperate
hearts

drifting
in
a drunkard's
dream,
mental constructions
making
silk purses
out of
pigs' ears
that disappear
with the craving
for the
next
distraction.

38

Did you
ever watch
electricity
fighting
against itself,
a destructive
application
of its
own true
nature
burning
down
the house—
can you
smell it?
and while
it is true
that
no
is an essential
part of yes
if it is
not seen
in the
perfect light
of intimate
space
it is
still only
a jailers
sweet
and tender
smile—my beloved,
you are
all the gardens
that I have
ever gazed at,
in your
renouncing
are you
truly there.

39

Winter
days always
reach
a point
when the
afternoon
fog
leaves its
nesting place
and crawls
over
the landscape;
form
and
outline
become
blurred,
unclear,
much like
the beasts
and
demons
that reside
in the
secret
unseen parts
of self
waiting
to be fed;
what must I
do
with this
vastness
that in the
open
defies
that which
would
sustain it.
I want to

spread
these words
like a blanket
over the
pieces of
me
that in silent
resting
hold each
other
in the
desire
to be whole.

40

Today
I went
out into
the backyard
and laid
down
on the
grass,
my eyes
grew heavy,
I could
smell the
homing
pigeons
(wishing
I didn't),
and hear the morning
doves in conversation
although
they seemed
to speak
different languages,
perhaps
it was merely
a matter
of dialect—
somewhere
through
all of this
conversation
I also was
listening
to the
Gulf of Mexico
and
I could
recognize
the waves
caressing
the shaved

headed
beach
with a
tender rhythm,
and just
for
a moment
I could
smell
the freedom
of sleep—
rolling over
I gasped
as my
heart crawled
out of
my chest
and placed
itself
in the shadow
where
I'm sure
that rest
sits looking.

41

I approach
some unseen
barrier,
a shadow,
or do I
simply imagine
too much,
attach too
much attention
to the clawing
inside my
conscience,
a method
of distraction
from the
uncertainty
of consequence
when
in fact,
what I would
really like
is to step
out of memory
so that I might
see more
clearly
the crying
child
that I loved
before
he was born—
the one
that I see
in all things
beautiful;
so tell
me,
where
is my place
in your

world
too often
shaped
by only
one
side of the
truth
at a time,
where "no"
sometimes
does
and sometimes
does not
possess its
own
character.

42

Thought
moves
delicately
through
my memory,
I observe
contact
with
form,
graceful
movements
flowing
through
an
imperceptible space
that is
my sense
self,
and out
of a corner
my eye
can
see
something
standing
at the place
where
the sea
and
beach
embrace each
other
publicly
in a pure
space
into which
nature's
love
is constantly expressed—
and in

the full
moon
of my soul-less
soul
there
is a howling.

43

I lay
on the couch
wondering
whether or not
I had
the inspiration
to walk
in and
out
of
the cracks
that sometimes
appear
in my
thinking;
I fell
asleep
wondering
how
you would
appear
in me
this night
of all nights,
wondering
if this moment
you
would
make your
bed
inside me
and dream
there;
I fell
asleep
wondering
if I
was strong
enough
to let go

of your
attention
for
that one
moment
which
wanted to
claim
me,
drag me
into
some fixed
notion
and
hold me
there,
a prisoner
until my
dreams
stopped
unable to
remember
their way
home.

44

When I
censor myself
too
sharply,
I wonder
if I have
ever been
been shamed,
I wonder
because
it is also
true
that
I would
rather not
talk
directly
to death,
somehow
thinking
that
I can
persuade
it
to act
differently,
but in the
end
it is
everywhere
full of
refusal
and I
strain
against
the weight
of that;
my body
is old
now

and
too many
times
broken
from chasing
after
my own
version
of things,
and I have
only
so many
breaths
left
and
yes
I would
give them
all
to you
to use
to climb
out
and
away from
the mystery
guest
that
keeps putting
a loaded gun
at the foot
of your
bed.

45

You
spoke to
me,
asked
to hear
more
directly
about the
war
that
lives on
in memory
as surely
as
the taste
of fried
bread
on a
cold winter
morning—
what can
you know
from
the night
sweats
that
soak
my dreams
in the smell
of too
fresh
blood—
mine,
mixed with
the young
and old
dead,
their intestines
hanging
out,

their genitals
now
in the wrong
place,
cut off
and
stuffed in
someones
mouth
instead of
hanging
just below
the navel
waiting to—
can you listen,
can you
step through
all the ideas
you ever
had
of
sanity,
of social rightness,
and listen
even when
you
want to
turn
away
or vomit,
because
I will tell
you—
and then
the
question
of love
will be
answered.

46

I
belong to
grief,
this is important
to know—
because who
is making
the decisions
when you
hold
them,
the others,
what are
you holding?
Do you tell
them,
who you
are?
do you tell
them
how much
of
their lives
you will eat?
do you allow
them to
enter
the private
places
of you,
deep inside,
and then
only let them
out
in the
solitude
that
casual
visitors
never see—

when you
hold
them,
what thoughts
occupy
you,
what images
are painted
behind
your eyes
closed,
and is it true
what you
said,
that
I can go
now—
if this
is so
then I
must admit,
I am afraid
to disappear.

47

Still,
quiet,
even
the Gulf
of Mexico,
wild as it
can be,
respects
this,
and I
come to
you
like all
the nights
before
to sit
between
the words
that define
this
union,
empty
of flesh.
I come
again
like all
the nights
before
to lay
beside you
without
shelter,
my
pockets
turned
inside out
so that
these
words
can fall

from
there place
of hiding
and
be
handed
over
to you
before
they
evaporate.

48

Rest
is often
too concentrated
on the
material,
on the
form
and function
of a
heart
in silence,
unstrung
and
scattered
like so
many
expensive things
laid aside
from
boredom,
never sure
and
wanting
to be—
last night
I was
so
concentrated
on the
material,
on the
form
and function,
that I
simply
could not
see
the
light
dancing

around
the room
offering
affection,
but
I heard
the
call
to me
or
wished it,
and
then all
the sounds
broke
apart
spilling
on the
blanket
of yet
another
restless
night,
waiting.

49

The
youngest
of us all
have
experienced
danger
and still
it is
so very hard
to hear
those violent
tones,
with a yet
undeveloped
ability
to listen,
that
somehow
seems
attractive—
the moth always
pursues
the
flame—
and how
does
this
fit,
skin
against
skin,
somehow
we
have always
known,
this
subtle
knowledge
acquired
by so

many
times
exposed
to the oblivion,
the desire
not to
feel—
and in
the end
does it
do
any good
to reveal
the
corners?

50

The shapes
that surround
me
form the
interpreted
space
that I
push against,
where
stars
fall
from the sky
right
through
the thickness
of touching,
without
contact,
the suchness
where
all
is—
so
here
just in this
space
senses
hide in
the abstract
of rivers,
waterfalls,
and great rooms
that have
ever layed
just
beyond
our sight,
perhaps
exactly
within

our foot steps;
so
just here
it is important
to remember,
(so may I
remind
you)
about
the
real effect
of
remembering,
it is important
to remember,
(so please
permit me)
to
look
on all the
imprisoned
images,
the ones
beyond
the edges,
like
too many
unpaid
debts
that hold
us defenseless;
and if
the remembering
is too painful,
throw
me out
into
empty space.
I'm sure
the forgetful

would like
that,
then
it will
all seem
somehow
easier
to hide
from
our
shared
breaths,
the silent
wind
that caresses
the
sun,
warming you
with tender
passion.

51

Dreams
possess
the smell
of confinement,
they pull at
me,
scratch
at my eyes
and tie
my feet
together.
If I am
able
I pick
myself up
from the
floor
and straighten
my clothes
in the
rushed
and
embarrassed
fashion
of a
young lover
discovered,
I rub
my hands
over my
shaved
head
straightening
the skin
curled
by the
strain
of too
many thoughts
pulling

at it—
is it ever
possible
to
save
another,
is it ever
possible
to save one's
self
from
oblivion,
from the
desire
not to feel,
constantly screaming
that it
is.

52

We are
not
close to
people
just because
we stand
next to them,
engage them
in conversation,
or lay
beside
them.
We are
not close
to people
just because
we hold
their physical
parts
in our hands
or mix them
with ours.
We look
on this
reflection
of holding
as our choice,
our reward,
while
unseen tensions
nag at
our desire
not to
and
in unison
drag us
deeper and deeper
into an
oblivion
shaped by

the
timeless mirror
of the
inherited,
the timeless
mirror
that reflects
everything
that is
the deception
of us,
while
we
are standing
just in front
unaware
and
crying
that it
might somehow
end
the need
to be
afflicted
because
it has
become
much
too heavy
and
at last
has sat on
our
chest
for far
too long.

53

A car
door slamming
is not
what we
perceive it
to be—
it simply
is
what it is;
our tendency
to escape
this,
so strong,
that we
cultivate
a
notion of
separation
endlessly,
dividing
it up
like so many
children do
when
picking sides
before
the games
start—
it is difficult
to take
life as it
is
with no fixed
points
to navigate
by
so we create
them,
body
and mind,

form and
emptiness,
mother,
daughter,
beloved, and
lover;
all this
is
about
keeping
a safe
distance.

54

What is
this
thing that
we call love,
this thing
that leaves
us with so
much tension,
that stands
up all
by itself
untouchable,
and with no
hands
chokes
the life
out of
so many—
observe
the
children,
beaten,
and those
who
have died
fighting
in the name
of you;
who is
this
then
that fly's
around
possessed of
shadowed
illness
always,
so near,
I want to
know

so I
am now
asking;
do you
sleep in me,
fill
every dream
that is
the scent
of a southern
cross
and
will I
awaken
in me,
to know
what I
can do
to interrupt
your
constant downfall?

55

Is it
likely
that once
found
I
would
hold
you too
close,
turn you
into
a secret,
or exploit
you
by becoming
me,
is it possible
that once
I found you
that
this silence
could stretch
out forever,
become
its own
morality
and I might,
in rapture,
miss
the trembling
truth
of contradiction,
miss
a piece of
life so new
that there
isn't yet
a name
for it,
a piece

of life
so new
that
those
looking
on
must
somehow
catch themselves
in
what
they ever
have seen,
the craving
for sequence,
a true
story
that never
happens—
yes,
those
looking on
will
generalize,
retreat
somehow
into
a social
sickness—
it
seems
easier
than holding
the awful
majesty
of everything
swirling
with rules
that were
never

bound,
and yet
somehow
are,
in the
pointless
point.

56

It is
in
the dark
places
between
tears,
where
I plead
with a
humid
silence
that
brings on
stillness
even to
the choirs
of frogs
whose
fragile
possibility
is to
serenade
the
thickness
of night,
announcing
their
presence
to their
predators
as all victims
do—
can we
generalize
about
such
a place,
where
almost
everything

is true,
a wilderness
that
comes on
hard
and
draws us
in,
where
invisible lips
speak to
us
and it
becomes necessary
to set
down
new
rules
about everything
we thought
we
knew.

57

You said
that you
wanted
to know
the truth
of it,
so
I will
tell you
about
war,
in the end
it won't
smell
like you
might
imagine,
and I
wonder
if you
really
want
the view
from
inside
the seams
of
my
experience,
the place
where
ideas
of ourselves
get
created,
and I
can not
prepare
you,
I can only

tell you
that
you will
taste
very distant,
that you
will
taste
abstract,
and
that
the dark
will
press
in
tight—
so,
when
I speak
to you
in this
special
dialect
will you
listen
like you
wanted
or will
you,
like
all the others,
tie my
tongue
in knots
and
then
shred
it
in little
pieces?

58

I can
yet
only
celebrate
a part
of your arrival,
just as every
thought
that
I could
notice you
enough—
beyond the
mystery
there
is no other
way
to do
this thing
that
is called
life
and survive,
there is
no sense
in asking
permission
to speak
directly,
then the
truth becomes
just a
shadow
of itself
always,
folding
into
a thick,
pasty
fog,

that steals
away
the ability
to take courage.

59

Most people
I know
don't
like
poetry
much—
of
the others
they
have too
many
ideas of
just how
all of this
is supposed
to work—
me,
I write
like this
because
I'm
scared
that
if I don't
the feeling
I
had
once
of being
alive
will melt again
into another one
of those
forgetful
moments
where
I actually
exist—
a moment
that

expands
and contracts
in the
space
between
the word—
letters
which,
fitted properly
together,
create
an existence
formed
of
realities
shaped and
cast
by the
many generations
past
that never are
absolutely
missing.

60

I sit here
alone
with only the
office light on.
It's late,
quiet everywhere
except
all through me,
nowhere to
trust,
not even the
loneliness
in front of me
echoing
the
sophisticated
manipulation
and
distortion
that is
a tightly
woven
carpet of morality
hidden
within layers
and layers
of white paste
that glues
a collage
of prescriptions
designed to
hide
and
hinder
the truth,
or any possibility
of reconstruction.

61

I was cruel
when
I was
younger,
I played
catch
with kittens—
I didn't
know
that they
were
like me,
alive—
or maybe
they weren't
because I
hadn't yet
discovered
our lives
have
the
same time
that they have,
theirs
quite
different from
mine
and yet
not—
the stillness
of their
breath
rhythms
remind me that
my time
and their
time
are not that
much different—
theirs is to

them
exactly
what
mine is
to me.

62

Getting up from
sitting
I am never sure
if my body
will co-operate—
there is
a price to be paid
for the endless
time between
then and
now,
a constant
struggle
to shape
the world
in an
image,
a reflection
of endless
empty efforts—
the floor
creaks
with each step
and my
mind
complains
about
the lack
of
co-operation—
then the
question:
will
all of this
appear
in the
world
before
it is
eaten?

63

Empty hearts,
steaks on
a grill,
eyes
shadowed
by
so much
beer
masquerading
as fun—
a wind
shift,
eyes stinging
from
barbecue breath,
a young
woman
appears
through
the tears,
her back
etched
with
the fine
lines
of
a corsette
tattoo,
the sight
of
which
begs for
stories
where
a
moment
becomes sharp,
clearly defined
and curious,
giving birth

to
imaginations
about
the
inspiration
to have
the laces
not yet
pulled
tight.

64

I was
thinking
about
my mother,
too often
lost
in a cascade
of dreams
that could
never
be,
consumed
by realities
that
were
by far
much stronger—
a
teenager
caught
in a web
where
no
did not hold
any substance,
or in fact
did not
exist,
even
as a
whisper—
how did it
happen
that I
was
born,
was there
any
choice
or is

there ever
any
choice?

65

When I
die
I would
like you
to
cry—
I would like
someone
to cry,
but isn't
this
just a bit
selfish—
and
if you cried
would that
really mean
that I was
important
to you,
to someone,
to anyone—
or wouldn't
it be
more real
if you
lived
your life
in a way
that
colored
everything
around you
with
the truth
that is
constantly
but so
seldom
seen

because of
a
too tight
grasping
at
shadows.

66

Where am I
in the
tree of
evolution,
how many
times
have I
been cut
down
and
refused
to die?
I sit
and
wonder,
is there
another
way
to give
back
oxygen?
I would,
you
know,
if I
were
permitted,
even
knowing
that
there
is
a
limited
supply—
I offered
it up
once,
all my
oxygen

and still
there
was
a constant
effort to
take more,
leaving me
abandoned
to daylight,
passed
out
in a doorway
with
the incense
of
vomit
filling
my
unholy sleep.

67

Random thoughts
appear
and then disappear
as quickly
as the news
of the
day,
but there is
always something
lingering
that is known,
if I dare
allow myself
to feel—
I mean really feel,
not think that I am.
Venturing into
this realm
of apparent
randomness
is a daunting
prospect that evades
conscious awareness
like a feral
cat
evades touch,
wanting it
but not trusting.
There are no
road signs
in this realm,
no sign posts,
traffic signals
or street lights—
no maps,
and still
everything can be seen
with eyes
shut,
a shimmering

that shows
a speed
that only anxiety
knows
if I dare to
embrace
it.
Awake,
I am silently asked,
what does one life
amount to?
Is there really an
answer to this?
Is one life worth more
than any other?
Sitting in this
pool of shimmering,
the question
wonders,
is there a specially
crafted
abacus
that can be used
to measure
the weight
of awareness,
and if so,
is there
a weight
limit
before
damage or
collapse?

68

There have been
those moments
when death
has
come on
quickly
with no time
to think
about
the transition,
even though
death
has a weight
to it,
at exactly
this moment
there can
only
be
acceptance—
when the
whole of
the experience
from beginning
to end
becomes pointless,
when death
lingers
whispering
picking at
you
in the night,
this is
another matter—
days
just
disappear
one into
the
next

and I
can't even
tell you
how quickly
the sharpness
of meaning
becomes
suddenly
quite dull.

69

My life
is
filled up
with details,
imperceptible
to most,
even to me
sometimes,
yet,
if I
miss one,
yes
just one,
life
begins
to spin
undetected,
unnoticed,
off its
axis.
Aware
of this,
or rather
wanting to
be,
I try
desperately
to not
miss
a single
point,
to think
about
them out loud,
but
this
exercise
is
in the

end
just
shadow-hunting.

70

I stood
in the
hall
just outside
a doorway,
the light
old
and soft
in behind.
I
was
making
an
attempt
to explain
or
rather describe
a
certain
flatness
that
takes
the very shape
of life
and turns
it
into a
shadow
of itself,
an echo
of
some
memory
that
perhaps
wasn't.
Thinking
all
the while
if

it could
be true
that
I simply
appeared
out of
nowhere.
Until now,
whenever
this
is,
I did
not know
that
learning
is
simply a
constant
movement
of ideas.

ABOUT THE AUTHOR

Claude AnShin Thomas is a decorated Vietnam combat veteran turned Zen Buddhist monk, author, and speaker. Claude AnShin communicates Zen Buddhist teachings in a non-religious manner that is direct and drawn from life, with a deep-rooted sense of compassion and purpose. He is the author of the award-winning book *At Hell's Gate: A Soldier's Journey from War to Peace* and more recently of *Bringing Meditation to Life: 108 Teachings on the Path of Zen Practice*.

International Work

Claude AnShin Thomas divides his time between the U.S., Europe, and South America, speaking about the real costs of war and violence and how meditation practice can support healing and transformation. He is dedicated to bringing awareness to the culture of violence in and among individuals, families, societies, and countries.

His intimate and deep understanding of the nature of suffering has allowed him to serve people in a wide variety of settings including war zones, hospitals, schools, and prisons. He has led meditation retreats at sites of war and suffering, and he communicates with gang members, guerrillas, and refugees. He offers public talks and retreats that help participants to recognize and end repetitive cycles of suffering.

Work with Veterans

Claude AnShin Thomas regularly leads meditation retreats for veterans living with post traumatic stress and moral injury. At these retreats, offered in locations around the U.S., veterans and their family members learn to practice meditation in a variety of forms including sitting, walking, working, eating, and writing, allowing them to begin the process of rebuilding their lives.

Academic Work

Claude AnShin Thomas has been a guest teacher and scholar-in-residence at Moravian College in Bethlehem, Pennsylvania, and Allegheny College in Meadville, Pennsylvania. Claude AnShin Thomas holds a BS in English Education from Slippery Rock University (Slippery Rock, PA), an MBA from Lesley University (Cambridge, MA), and an honorary Doctorate in Divinity from Moravian College (Bethlehem, PA).

ALSO AVAILABLE

At Hell's Gate: A Soldier's Journey from War to Peace

In this raw and moving memoir, Claude AnShin Thomas describes his service in Vietnam, his subsequent emotional collapse, and his remarkable journey toward healing. "Everyone has their Vietnam," Thomas writes. "Everyone has their own experience of violence, calamity, or trauma."

This book offers timeless teachings on how we can all find healing, with practical guidance on how mindful awareness and compassion can transform our lives.

"Claude Anshin Thomas has been an inspiration to me. Our world urgently needs to listen to him tell of his life in war and then in peace."
—Maxine Hong Kingston, author of *The Woman Warrior*

"Written with relentless courage and utter compassion, this account of violence and transformation is one of the most amazing and wonderful stories I've ever read."

—Michael Herr, Vietnam War correspondent and author of *Dispatches*

Bringing Meditation to Life: 108 Teachings on the Path of Zen Practice

Presented in 108 short, to-the-point, provocative chapters, this book offers essential instruction on sitting meditation practice and how it can inform our relationships, communication, conflicts, peace work, and more. Interspersed throughout the book are some of the author's favorite quotes from Zen literature.

"Claude AnShin distills the wisdom he has earned through the practice of meditation and a remarkable life devoted to the dharma, peacemaking, and serving others. This is a book, and a rare teacher, worthy of our trust."
—Charles Johnson, winner of the National Book Award and author of *Turning the Wheel: Essays on Buddhism and Writing*

'Shorn of mystification and cultural accretions, this is an elegant book which I recommend to students new to Zen and to those who wish to go deeper."
—Hozan Alan Senauke, abbot of Berkeley Zen Center, author of *The Bodhisattva's Embrace: Dispatches from Engaged Buddhism's Front Lines*

'This book is a must read for anyone walking the path of peace and justice."
—Genjo Marinello, abbot of Chobo-ji Zen Temple, Seattle

Printed by Amazon Italia Logistica S.r.l.
Torrazza Piemonte (TO), Italy

61350828R00079